The Wounded Yellow Butterfly

Lost

3 4028 08799 1916
HARRIS COUNTY PUBLIC LIBRARY

J Diaz
Diaz, Linda
The wounded yellow
butterfly : a story of
loss, friendship and hope
$12.00
ocn918895763
08/18/2015

D0731995

Illustrated
by
Timothy Banks

A story
of loss,
friendship
and hope

Linda Díaz, LPC, CTS, RPT

Copyright © 2014 Linda Diaz, LPC, CTS, RPT
All rights reserved.
ISBN: 0615761399
ISBN 13: 9780615761398
Library of Congress control number: 2013902047
Linda\Díaz-Murphy
North Charleston, South Carolina

Dedication

This book is dedicated to my loving husband Brian Martin who faces all life's challenges with gusto and bravery and who makes me feel loved. To my daughters Anais Rachel and Michelle Arianna who inspire me constantly, and are the quintessence of light, hope, kindliness and beauty. To my son-in-law John William, who teaches us all how to be grateful. To my amazing grandchildren, Morgan Michelle (who contributed thoughtful and creative feedback for the illustrations) and John "Moose" (who came up with the caterpillar character for this book). You are both the embodiment of peace and love. I love you!

Words of Gratitude

I wish to express my deep affection and profound gratitude to Dr. Ronald Murphy for lighting my path through my personal storm and for teaching me the way of the wounded healer.

I want to give a special thank you to Barbara Maurer who has mentored me at different stages of my profession in helping others recover from traumatic loss.

To the children and their families who persevered, I wish to express my indebtedness for allowing me to come along on their healing journeys.

It was a beautiful day in the peaceful garden. At the entrance of the garden, there were orange trumpet flowers hanging from the tall arbor that called visitors to the garden. Purple, pink, and blue morning glories had opened and were hung along the white winding gate that surrounded the garden. Bright red, yellow, and pink flowers were budding, while various other flowers had already blossomed. There was a purple butterfly bush in full bloom in the peaceful garden. The monarch butterfly, a yellow butterfly, two bees, one moth, two wasps, and one mosquito were soaring from one flower to the next, suckling the juices of each flower. A worm stuck his head out from the ground and smiled as it looked around the garden.

There was a beautiful water garden with a small, natural cascading waterfall. Glass gazing balls that decorated the peaceful garden mirrored the sun and the blue sky. Several caterpillars were crawling up the side of a red one-car garage toward the branches of the largest apple tree one can't imagine.

A white, wooden swinging chair for two hung from one of the apple tree's seven strong branches. The tree was home to a nest with three baby bluebirds without any feathers; and the mother bluebird and the father bluebird. Two squirrels were hugging, laughing, and smiling while they played in the garden. Nearby, the skunk family was having fun, too. The yellow butterfly said, "This is a beautiful day in the peaceful garden."

ater that day dark clouds formed and covered the sun and the blue sky. The monarch butterfly, a yellow butterfly, two bees, one moth, two wasps, one mosquito, two squirrels, the blue bird family, the caterpillars, the skunk family and the worm stopped and looked up at the darkening sky with surprise. The peaceful garden insects and the animals became paralyzed with fear when the light from the sun completely disappeared. The yellow butterfly said, "This has turned into an unbelievable day."

Gusts of wind created cyclones of green leaves and garbage that flew through the once-peaceful garden. The squirrels ran into a burrow for safety, but that was soon flooded by torrential rain. The squirrels then ran through the door of the red-brick garage and huddled together inside the dark garage.

The monarch butterfly, a yellow butterfly, two bees, one moth, two wasps, and one mosquito linked wings and hid in the purple butterfly bush, until it was too windy to hold on any longer. The bluebirds sunk deep into their nest. The worm hid its head in the ground. The caterpillars crawled into an open garage window for shelter. The skunk family found refuge in a garbage can that had flown into the garden. The skunks' eyes widened with fear as they watched other garbage cans roll on the ground and fly through the air. The yellow butterfly said, "This has turned into the scariest day ever."

The day after the storm, the once-peaceful garden was a terrible sight to see. The wind had blown garbage from nearby homes into the garden. The glass gazing balls that had decorated the garden were shattered. The waterfall was damaged. Many flowers were bent or broken at their stems. The purple butterfly bush that once protected and fed the monarch butterfly, a yellow butterfly, two bees, one moth, two wasps, and one mosquito was pulled halfway out of the ground. Lightning had struck the apple tree, cracking one of its limbs. This frightened the bluebird family whose nest sat on a nearby branch. The squirrels, who had run into the garage for safety, now felt sad as they looked through the window at the damaged garden. The yellow butterfly said, "This is a miserable day."

On the fourth day after the storm, the sun came out and gleamed through the light-gray clouds, illuminating the garden. The insects and animals began to come out of their shelters. There was pain in their hearts as they looked around the garden. One of the skunks noticed that the yellow butterfly was wounded and screamed, "Look at the yellow butterfly! It has lost parts of both its wings." The monarch butterfly, two bees, one moth, two wasps, and one mosquito, the worm who brought a kindhearted friend along, two skunks, the mother blue bird, and the two squirrels were angry to see the two torn wings on the yellow butterfly. The wounded yellow butterfly said, "This is a 'why me?' day."

On the fifth day after the storm, the monarch butterfly, two bees, one moth, two wasps, one mosquito, two squirrels, the blue bird family, the caterpillars, the skunk family and the worm began to clean up the garden. Despite having injured wings, the wounded yellow butterfly was able to help clean up the garden with the others and thought that some of the garbage was recyclable. The wounded yellow butterfly said, "This is cleanup day."

The wounded yellow butterfly sifted through the garbage and uncovered a cardboard paper towel tube and had an idea and excitedly said, "Let's all make a kaleidoscope." The wounded yellow butterfly colored the paper towel tube yellow using the pistils from the white daisies. The skunk family gathered silver foil and placed it inside the paper towel tube to reflect light from the sun.

The two squirrels then put the beautiful and colorful bits of glass from the broken glass gazing balls between two pieces of cellophane and placed it carefully at the top end of the cardboard paper towel tube.

The monarch butterfly, two bees, one moth, two wasps, and one mosquito wrapped a blue ribbon around the top of the tube to hold the cellophane in place, while a good-natured caterpillar ate through the bottom of the tube, making an eyehole in the middle to look through.

Then the monarch butterfly, two bees, one moth, two wasps, and one mosquito tied a beautiful bow with the blue ribbon that held the cellophane around the top end of the paper towel roll.

Once the kaleidoscope was completed, the squirrels and skunks held the bottom of the kaleidoscope while the monarch butterfly, two bees, one moth, two wasps, and one mosquito tried lifting the top part of the kaleidoscope toward the sun. But the kaleidoscope was too heavy, and it fell back to the ground. The wounded yellow butterfly wanted to help lift the kaleidoscope but thought it would be impossible to ever fly again. The wounded yellow butterfly said, "This is a challenging day."

Mysteriously, the wounded yellow butterfly gathered up a lot of courage, and with great determination, flew up toward the blue sky and warm sun to hold up the kaleidoscope along with the monarch butterfly, two bees, one moth, two wasps, and one mosquito. Everyone cheered, "Hooray!"

E veryone was curious and got a chance to look into the kaleidoscope. As the animals and insects took turns rotating and looking through the eyehole of the kaleidoscope, the light entering the top end created never-ending vibrant colorful designs.

The following morning, as the wind blew softly through the peaceful garden, the sound of a wind chime that now hung from the new branch of the apple tree was heard by all in the garden. The monarch butterfly, the wounded yellow butterfly, two bees, one moth, two wasps, one mosquito, two squirrels, the blue bird family, the caterpillars, the skunk family and the worm paused to listen to the wind chime, and remembered of things past for a brief moment. The wounded yellow butterfly said, "This is remembrance day."

It was a sunny day in the peaceful garden. At the entrance of the garden, there were orange trumpet flowers hanging from the tall arbor that called visitors to the garden. Purple, pink, and blue morning glories had opened and were hung along the white winding gate that surrounded the garden. Bright red, yellow, and pink flowers were budding, while various other flowers had already blossomed. There was a purple butterfly bush in full bloom in the garden. The monarch butterfly, the wounded yellow butterfly, two bees, one moth, two wasps, and one mosquito were soaring from one flower to the next, suckling the juices of each flower. Five new dazzling butterflies emerged from their cocoons and joined in the fun. A worm stuck his head out from the ground and smiled as it looked around the garden.

There was a beautiful water garden with a small, natural cascading waterfall. Glass gazing balls that decorated the peaceful garden mirrored the sun and the blue sky. A couple of caterpillars were crawling up the side of a red one-car garage toward the branches of the largest apple tree one can't imagine.

The two squirrels were hugging, laughing, and smiling while they swung on the white, wooden swinging chair for two hanging from one of the apple tree's seven strong branches. In the peaceful garden the three young blue birds with beautiful blue feathers played while the mother and father blue birds sat contentedly on a branch in the apple tree. Nearby, the skunk family was having fun, too. The wounded yellow butterfly said, "This is a new day in the peaceful garden."

How can
The Wounded Yellow Butterfly
story help children?

The Wounded Yellow Butterfly story is about healing after a fierce storm. The story helps children of any age express feelings associated with traumatic loss and grief stemming from natural disasters, war, terrorism, bullying, foster care placement, loss of classmate, pet loss, abuse, terminal illness, divorce, the death of a sibling or other family member, environmental contamination or other countless traumatic events. Traumatic loss may destroy the idea in a child's mind that the world is a safe place. Traumatic experiences affect children's sense of control, trust, and hope for the future. The story of the wounded yellow butterfly helps parents to better understand the grief process while providing a comforting way for children to learn to cope with loss. The wounded yellow butterfly guides children through the grief process and toward the transformation to hopefulness by providing them with a way to regain trust, express and cope with their feelings, a safe way to tell their story of loss, and aid with the reconnection to others. The story of the wounded yellow butterfly aids children everywhere through trauma, recovery and eventual triumph.

H ere are a few questions one might ask children to help them identify feelings such as joy, horror, fear, sadness, anger, loss, courage, hope, and triumph. The questions can also help show children that they might need someone else to help them through the storm and that they can offer help to others:

A. What do you think the butterflies, animals, and insects felt before the storm? During the storm? After the storm?

B. How do you think the insects and animals felt when the wounded butterfly thought of making the kaleidoscope?

C. How do you think the butterfly felt and thought when it looked through the kaleidoscope?

D. Have you ever been in a storm or experienced something scary? Describe your experience.

E. Who and/or what do you trust in, when you are in a fierce storm, that makes you feel safe rather than afraid?

The meaning of *The Wounded Butterfly*:

- *The Wounded Butterfly* normalizes for children what may be experienced after a storm or some other traumatic event.

- The garbage provides a symbolic representation of things or thoughts that a child may want or need help recycling, reframing, or getting rid of to allow him or her to move from trauma to recovery.

- The wounded yellow butterfly is a metaphor for the pain or injury children experience and live with but can overcome. Depending on others is also encouraged. This is represented by the fact that the wounded yellow butterfly, the animals and other insects can rely on each other to rebuild their lives.

- The kaleidoscope is a metaphor for change. Each time the kaleidoscope rotates, a new combination of colors and shapes appear aiding us in looking at things in different ways. We can change our thoughts, feelings, and actions just as a kaleidoscope changes designs.

- *The Wounded Butterfly* helps act from a place of hope rather than fear.

Acknowledgments

I would like to pay tribute to the many people I have met along my professional journey and the organization to which they belong who freely give their love, time, and resources to helping children and their families recover from traumatic loss and grief. Special Thanks go to Marjorie Aldama, Donna Amundson, Nancy Baird, Renee Burawski, Shauntay Campbell, Mark Chaves, Deb Brodt-Donnelly, Donna Drummond, David Fahy, Sue Haguy, Cheryl Hurst, Jodi Kosofsky, Mary Pat McGeehan, Gretchen Morgan, Beatriz Reyes, Dotty Rodrick, Cara Natale Ruddy, Jessica Shea, Alyson Smith, Meg Clark Soriano, Diane Freiermuth Travers, and Mayra Velez.

The Traumatic Loss Coalitions for Youth

The dual mission of the TLC is excellence in suicide prevention and trauma and promoting post trauma healing and resiliency for the youth of New Jersey.

Go to the TLC *website* for more on grief support programs for children and teens, suicide prevention, mental health organizations and other international, national and local programs and services.
Tel: 732-235-2810
ubhc.rutgers.edu/brti/tlc

The Association of Traumatic Stress Specialists

The mission of the Association of Traumatic Stress Specialists (ATSS) is to organize, educate, and professionally certify our world-wide membership in order to assist those affected by trauma.
Tel: 864-294-4337

<u>**www.atssa.com**</u>

National Child Traumatic Stress Network (NCTSN)
<u>http://wwwnctsnet.org</u>

New Jersey Disaster Mental Health Services (NJDMHS)

The Disaster and Terrorism Branch has created a brochure addressing the impact of storms and flooding, as well as strategies for coping. You can download the brochure to learn more about how to manage the emotional impact of a severe storm or flood.
<u>http://www.state.nj.us/humanservices/dmhs/disaster/</u>

New Jersey MentalHealthCares Helpline
1-866-202-4357

A New Jersey's mental health information and referral service.
<u>http://www.njmentalhealthcares.org</u>

NJ Rainbows

An international, not-for-profit organization that fosters emotional healing among children grieving a loss from a life-altering crisis.
www.rainbows.org

The Lighthouse Counseling & Sand Play Training Center provides counseling to families and children suffering traumatic loss, and Sand Play training to professionals who help families reduce the effects of trauma on their lives.

Lighthouse Counseling & Sand Play Training Center
615 Hope Road, Bldg. 3A
Eatontown, NJ 07724
Phone: 732-380-1575 xt. 301
Fax: 732-380-1578
Contact: Gretchen Morgan
gmorgan@lcsnj.com
www.lcsnj.com

Special Thanks

Special thanks go to the CreateSpace team, who made this book a reality. I am especially thankful to Timothy for the very beautiful illustrations he created for this book. I am grateful to John Mark Schuster, Christine, Stewart, Anna and many others for their guidance and patience. Thank you for making it possible for this wonderful wounded yellow butterfly story to reach children and their families who need support through their personal storms.

Resource

Kaleidoscopes To You
Kaleidoscope Toys & Kits
Phone Karl and Jean Schilling at 641-454-2068
karl@kaleidoscopestoyou.com
www.kaleidoscopestoyou.com

Donation

10% of the proceeds from the sale of this book will go to buy a book for a child, library, school or organization helping children recover from traumatic loss.

If you wish to donate a book, please contact Linda Díaz at woundedyellowbutterfly@gmail.com